Roger Hutchison

THE
Very
Best
DAY

The Way of Love
for Children

Foreword by Jerusalem Jackson Greer

CHURCH
PUBLISHING
INCORPORATED

Church Publishing
19 East 34th Street
New York, NY 10016
www.churchpublishing.org

Cover design by: Lorraine Simonello
Typeset by: Beth Oberholtzer

A record of this book is available from the Library of Congress.

ISBN-13: 9781640652811 (pbk.)
ISBN-13: 9781640652828 (ebook)

To the young boy who asked,
"Why were you searching for me?
Did you not know that I must be
in my Father's house?"

This book is my humble gift to you.

You **are** the *way of love*.

Presented to

_____

From

_____

On the occasion of

_____

Date

_____

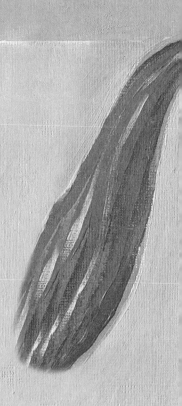

Foreword

In the spring of 2018, a group of formation leaders—clergy and lay—in the Episcopal Church gathered together in a room on the campus of Virginia Theological Seminary. Our task, handed to us by Presiding Bishop Michael Curry, was to create a set of spiritual practices that would help people—from ages 5 to 95—live a Jesus-centered life in practical and sacred ways. The Way of Love, with its seven practices, is what emerged.

Our work that weekend felt both holy and radical. (Why do those things so often seem to go together?) In an era of declining church attendance, we were daring to believe that this work might just matter; people were hungry to know how to live a Jesus-centered life, following his way of love no matter who they were or what their circumstances may be.

And so we wrote and we prayed and we sang, we worshiped and we wrote some more. We wrote out of our own experiences, our own longings to follow Jesus more closely. We wrote from the questions we had heard from around the church: what did it really mean to live as Jesus movement people? We wrote from our tradition, we wrote from scripture, we wrote from prayer. And then we gave the work to God and to the church, to grow and to multiply. The Way of Love is no more proprietary than the love of Jesus is proprietary. It is freely given, and it can be freely built upon. And wow, did it grow!

Over the past year it has been absolutely delightful to see the resources that volunteers, youth ministers, Sunday school teachers, bishops, and priests from across the Church have created to support the Way of Love practices. From a Way of Love spinner game to a body prayer and so much more in between, formation leaders have done an amazing job at helping all ages learn how to live a Jesus-centered life. But the Way of Love is not just for churches; it is also for individuals and families. It is not just meant for Sunday mornings; it is also meant for Friday nights and Tuesday afternoons—we are called to love and serve Christ no matter where we are or what we are doing.

And now we have Roger's beautiful book. I don't know which I love more—his words or his images (and that says a lot because Roger's images are just gorgeous). This is a book that needs to be read out loud multiple times, and it is a book for feasting on with your eyes for hours of contemplation. Roger has captured the essence of the Way of Love beautifully, while diving even deeper into what it means to live and love like Jesus in the beautiful, sacred, everyday moments of life. It is a book that can be read to start the day or end the day, a book that can be read at church and on the soccer field, in a classroom and in the car.

Write these commandments that I've given you today on your hearts. Get them inside of you and then get them inside your children. Talk about them wherever you are, sitting at home or walking in the street; talk about them from the time you get up in the morning to when you fall into bed at night. Tie them on your hands and foreheads as a reminder; inscribe them on the doorposts of your homes and on your city gates. (Deuteronomy 6:8–9, The Message)

The Very Best Day is a gift of a book—one that can help teach the gifts of the Way of Love to children of all ages, providing a model for what it means to live, and move, and have their being in Jesus and his way of love—when they feel sad, when they feel glad, in the morning, in the evening, at school, and at play.

I pray that you will wear your copy of this book out as you grow in grace, following Jesus and his way of love.

Jerusalem Jackson Greer
Staff Officer for Evangelism for the Episcopal Church
Preservation Acres, Arkansas

Turn

On warm spring days,
  when the sky is pale
  blue,
I pull on my boots and
  go to the flower garden
  with you.
We pick some flowers;
  I choose a pink one,
  and you, a white.
We begin to dance and
  laugh with delight.
We fill a vase with water
  that is cool to the
  touch,
Almost to the top, but
  not too much.
In go the flowers,
  "Be gentle!" you say.
This has been
  a colorful day.

Night falls softly, and I say a prayer.
I give thanks for the garden
and you taking me there.
Thanks for my family, the sunlight,
and Jesus' love.
I drift off to sleep as the stars twinkle above.

What ways do I grow when
I turn toward Jesus' love?

Learn

I awake to light filling my room.
The smiling sun replaced the quiet moon.
It's a new day, and I am ready to learn!
How ice freezes . … what makes a fire burn?
We learn new things when awake and falling asleep.
We even learn when counting sheep.

We learn at school, at church, and on the playground.
We learn about the earth and what makes it go around.
It's not always easy, I want to give in.
I must work hard and try again and again.
At the farm we learn about horses, cows, and hay.
This has been **a growing day**.

We learn about Jesus,
his miracles, and his love.
We learn that God sent him
from above.

How can you learn
more about Jesus
and his love?

pray

When thankful or afraid, I say a prayer.
I know in my heart that Jesus is there.
With hands raised high or down on my knees,
I cry out and he calms the rough seas.

Sometimes I hurt and want to hide.
I'm not alone, he's by my side.
Jesus always loves me and shows me the way.
This has been **an emotional day**.

At a table, his friends were gathered there,
With gentleness and love he taught them this prayer:

Our Father, who art in heaven,
hallowed be thy Name,
thy kingdom come,
thy will be done,
on earth as it is in heaven.
Give us this day our daily bread.
And forgive us our trespasses,
as we forgive those
who trespass against us.
And lead us not into temptation,
but deliver us from evil.
For thine is the kingdom,
and the power, and the glory,
for ever and ever. Amen.

When do you pray? What do you say when you talk to God?

Worship

On Sunday morning I go to church with family
   and friend.
The song of the bells carried on the wind.
We sing, we pray, we bow our head.
With hands outstretched, we receive the bread.
He gave his life so that we might live.
It's his love and peace that we must give.
The greeters and ushers show us the way.
This has been
   a holy day.

Sometimes we kneel, more often we stand.
After worship we play, our clothes covered in sand.
There is time for Sunday school and snack.
We learn about Jesus' miracles, I can't wait to come back!
Worship is holy, it's special and good.
Want to come with me? I think you should.

What is your favorite part of worship? Why?

Bless

Some days I'm so happy, I feel my heart might burst.
Other days I'm sad and angry. Those are the worst.
You give me a hug and remind me you're here.
I cuddle in close and even shed a tear.
A hug, a smile, an enormous grin.
Love like Jesus, and you'll feel peace within.
Meeting someone new takes focus and work.
It's hard to be a friend with a frown or a smirk.
Be generous, be kind, and invite them to play.
This has been **a loving day**.

The **way of love** is the path we must go.
We know this because Jesus tells us so.
Be a blessing, a joy, a good listener.
You, my child, are Jesus' missioner.

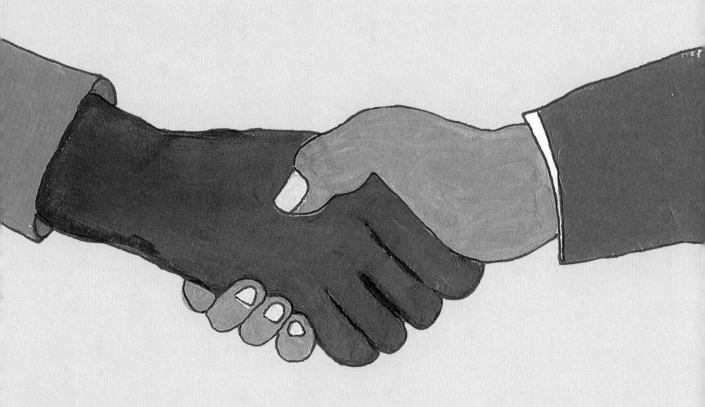

You are a blessing. Can you name the ways?

Go

"Go in peace to love and serve the Lord," the priest will say.
The heavy doors open, and we are sent on our way.
To home, to school, and to work we must go.
Spreading his love so that others will know.
Sharing stories of healing, baskets of fish, and mother Mary.
Never forget the heavy cross that Jesus did carry.
We run, we jump, we stumble along the way.
This has been **an active day**!

Lace up those shoes, and tie them on tight.
Be strong, be bold, don't give up the fight.
Jesus' love is needed all around the earth.
Our lives changed forever on the day of his birth.
"Thanks be to God!" our words fill the air.
"Ready, set, **go**, I'll race you there!"

What does "Go in peace to love and serve the Lord" mean to you?

Rest

God created the earth, the moon, and the sun.
Blue whales that swim and spotted cheetahs that run.
Day one, day two, day three, and day four.
Wait! God's not finished, there are still a few more.
Day five and day six, the beauty of creation.
Birds of every color, people of every nation.
Day one through day seven, God said, "This is good."
Then God rested like you and I should.
Deep breaths, meditation, and peaceful play.
This has been **a relaxing day**.

When we don't slow down, close our eyes, and rest,
We are weak, overwhelmed, and not at our best.
We've got work to do, and that takes energy.
It's part of life's rhythm for you and for me.

What do you do to slow down and rest?

Jesus is love, this is clear.
God walks among us and holds us near.
We **turn** toward the Light, we grow, and we change.
Some days full of wonder, some days just strange.
We **learn** when we listen, practice, and read.
Stories of Jesus teach us the skills that we need.
We **pray** the Lord's Prayer, like Jesus taught us to do.
You pray for me, and I pray for you.

We gather together to **worship** God's Son.
He is strength and might and loves us—each one.
We **bless** one another with our joy and our smiles,
Whether we live near each other
  or across many miles.
We **go** through those doors to love and to serve.
To feed, to comfort, to calm an anxious nerve.
Then we must slow down, relax, and **rest**.
Life can be a struggle, life can be a test.
Jesus has taught us that love is the way.
I hope you have **the very best day**.

A Note from the Author

At the 79th General Convention of the Episcopal Church in July 2018, Presiding Bishop Michael B. Curry called the Church to practice the Way of Love. It was an invitation to all of us, young and old alike, to "grow more deeply with Jesus Christ at the center of our lives, so we can bear witness to his way of love in and for the world."[1]

The Very Best Day is a book for children. In writing this book, my primary goal was to write engaging and inspiring poetry that will not only encourage children to read but will also provide the language and framework for identifying and establishing a "rule of life."

Through accessible language and vibrant color, I hope the ancient rhythm of our story unfolds for you and your child. It is imperative, especially in the atmosphere of the world we live in today, that we provide opportunities for our children to discover and experience these holy practices and rhythms at an early age so that they are able to flourish as healthy teenagers and adults. I can't imagine a better way to do this than to wonder and walk together with Jesus and the Way of Love.

Roger Hutchison
Houston, Texas

---

1. You can learn more about the Way of Love, including an invitation from Presiding Bishop Michael Curry, at www.episcopalchurch.org/way-of-love.